WHEN THEY
COME HOME

*Ways to welcome
returning Catholics*

WHEN THEY COME HOME

Ways to welcome returning Catholics

MELANIE RIGNEY AND
ANNA M. LANAVE

TWENTY
THIRD 23rd
PUBLICATIONS
www.23rdpublications.com

Second printing 2011

TWENTY-THIRD PUBLICATIONS
A Division of Bayard
One Montauk Avenue, Suite 200
New London, CT 06320
(860) 437-3012 or (800) 321-0411
www.23rdpublications.com

ISBN 978-1-58595-761-3
Library of Congress Catalog Card Number: 2009936460
Printed in the U.S.A.

Contents

ACKNOWLEDGMENTS

When you get involved in ministering to the returning Catholic, you may witness your share of miracles. The development of the book you are holding is also a small miracle. We would be remiss if we didn't show our gratitude:

ANNA: I thank my husband, Gregory LaNave. As a stay-at-home mom of four young children who is called to minister to working adults, I can't thank Greg enough for the countless evenings of "kid duty." I am able to be a loving presence to others because of the unwavering love and support he has shown me. I also thank Lucia, Dominic, Antonio, and Vincent for all the kisses I receive as I head out the door to church to "tell people about Jesus." Thank you for sharing your mom with others.

MELANIE: So many people have played roles in my faith journey. In particular, I'd like to thank Ann Pulliam, who was on the *Landings* team when I went through the program; my best friend, Patricia Lorenz; and the Arlington Diocese Cursillo Community, especially the great women in my prayer groups.

We both would like to acknowledge the Rev. Gerry Creedon, pastor of St. Charles Borromeo Catholic Church in Arlington, Virginia. Thank you for identifying and the empowerment of the gifts of the members of the parish to minister to each other. Thank you that you care about inactive Catholics enough to nurture a returning Catholics program and to be always available to help reconcile people to the Church. You truly shepherd your people with care.

Finally, we thank the St. Charles *Landings* ministry, the team members who have given themselves to this quiet ministry and the returnees who have shared their stories. We hope their experiences can truly bless and inspire you.

INTRODUCTION

[Jesus] said to him the third time, "Simon, son of John, do you love me?" Peter was distressed that he had said to him a third time, "Do you love me?" and he said to him, "Lord, you know everything; you know that I love you." [Jesus] said to him, "Feed my sheep." JOHN 21:17

A program for returning Catholics may be the most profound, rewarding ministry your parish has undertaken.

As a pastor, parish staffer, or lay leader, you doubtless have found comfort in your faith and community during some of life's biggest challenges. You know the strength the Eucharist and the Great Amen provide, the peace of reconciliation, and the joy that comes with witnessing or experiencing the rites of baptism, confirmation, and matrimony.

Now, imagine someone who is Catholic by virtue of baptism and confirmation, but away from those gifts God gives us, sometimes for decades. The reason for his or her departure may have seemed important at the time—wanting to sleep in on Sundays, not "getting anything" out of Mass, not feeling welcome at the parish, not wanting to go to Mass alone, or not understanding some of our faith's doctrines and dogma.

There are forty million "away" Catholics in the United States. It's certain that something—marriage, birth, death, divorce—will bring some of them to your parish door, tentative and hungry.

1

How will you feed them?

This book's goal is to give you the tools you need to set up a short course for these sheep who have already begun the reconversion process at some level.

Chapter 1, "The Missing Sheep," provides a snapshot of these "away" Catholics and the reasons (some of which will surprise you) that they are inactive. We also explain why at this juncture of the Church's life in the United States it is especially important that we reach out to inactives.

In Chapter 2, "Preparing the Pasture," we offer tips for preparing your parish, including staff, to welcome returnees, whether they make their entrance in a program or as "newcomers" seeking the sacraments.

Chapter 3, "How to Help Them Find You," provides strategies for letting returnees know they are welcome in your parish. This chapter has a strong emphasis on Internet strategies, but also offers templates for bulletin and pulpit announcements.

Once returnees have found you, it's important to see whether your program is right for them—and vice versa. Chapter 4, "The Meeting," shares likely questions and suggests structure for the meeting.

Chapter 5, "Building Your Program and Team," outlines the formal and informal approaches to programs. You'll find a basic topic schedule as well as thoughts on selecting your lay leader and team members.

For a session-by-session discussion guide, including questions you're likely to hear, check out Chapter 6, "Feeding the Flock."

In Chapter 7, "Feeding Their Fire," we share some suggestions for helping the returnees channel their rekindled passion into ministries at your parish and beyond.

An appendix provides information about existing programs and services parishes can use as well as Web links of interest to the lay leaders and returnees.

Along the way, we share the snapshots of the journeys of real-life returnees—including the two of us—as well as tips for success developed during nearly a decade of ministry to returnees.

No matter which strategy your parish chooses—homegrown or adoption of an existing program such as Catholics Coming Home, Catholics Returning Home, or Landings—your program doesn't have to cost much: some photocopying of handouts, a room once a week for twelve or so weeks per year; a few hours of volunteers' time. God will take care of the rest.

Open your heart. Open your arms. Open your soul. Feed his sheep.

CHAPTER 1

The Missing Sheep

"I was baptized Catholic, but my parents did it for my grandparents and we never went to Mass or CCD..."

"I was raised in a strong Catholic home, Mass every Sunday, but when I got to college, I just stopped going. It just didn't mean anything to me."

"I used to be Catholic, but I married a non-Catholic..."

It's the "but" that tears at the heart. Those of us who love our Catholic faith have heard these words too many times. These inactive Catholics are all around us: the woman at the playground who looks wistful when you talk about the local parish school; the coworker who jokes when he observes you not eating meat on a lenten Friday; the next-door neighbor who waves and watches you drive away to Mass on Sunday mornings while he mows the grass.

But these statements and interactions offer hope for a re-kindled relationship with Christ and our Church. People like those in the examples still identify with some part of their lost Catholicism; many consider themselves "still Catholic," and that is something.

As a parish staff member, you may see the "but" almost every day. They are the young couple who come to find out about a church wedding, mainly to please their parents, and are surprised to learn that they must attend marriage preparation. They are the couples who call about scheduling a baptism and don't understand why at least one godparent has to be a practicing Catholic. They are the grieving middle-aged daughters and sons who quit coming to Mass a long time ago, but know their parents would want a proper Catholic burial.

You do your best to help them, of course, but it's hard. Their knowledge of the faith and their relationship with Christ and the Church appears to be limited at best, and your parish's needs are many. Why should your parish expend resources on people who aren't regularly in the pews?

The answer is simple.

Because this is the essence of being Christian. The Good Shepherd loves all his own, and we, as his followers, are called to extend his mercy and love to those who have drifted away. The shepherd who went after that one missing sheep...the father of the prodigal son...the vineyard owner who paid the men he hired late in the day the same wage he paid the early workers. Those are the people he calls us to emulate.

Catholicism is a communal faith, lived out through the local parish. We are incomplete without these Catholics. The body of Christ needs to have them back with us, contributing their talents and treasures to building the kingdom. We yearn to see this group of people back in the fold and living an active Catholic life. It is a blessing to be a guide and witness in warmly welcoming inactives who come to the parish office because of life events such as baptism, marriage, or the death of a loved one. The Holy Spirit may be using this opportunity to change a life or two, and you can be part of that miracle.

Wherever your parish is located, it's a sure bet there are a whole lot of people missing from your pews. According to the Center for Applied Research in the Apostolate (CARA) at Georgetown University, there are close to sixty-five million Catholics in the United States. Of those, only thirty-six percent attend Mass on a weekly basis (CARA's measure of an active Catholic). That means nearly two-thirds are inactive— over forty million people—but still call themselves "Catholic." (This group, inactive Catholics, is the second largest "Church" in the country.)

Why You Need Them

Twenty years ago, studies confirmed something the Church has always found consoling: even though forty-two percent of all Catholics traditionally were inactive for at least two years in their teens and twenties, an estimated fifty percent came back as they married and had children.

But as our society changes, so does the Church. According to the 2008 CARA report, the median age for having left the Catholic faith is increasing. From 1953 to 1962, the median age was seventeen; from 1993 to 2002, it was twenty-six. This change is significant because the later people leave the Church, the less likely they are to come back.

Further, as ethnic Catholics have assimilated into the American society, their demographics now mirror that of the general population. The increase in Catholics marrying non-Catholics, people marrying much later in life, and the breakdown of Catholicism rooted in ethnicity have all lessened the likelihood of a natural return to the Church.

About the "But"

There are many reasons why people stop practicing Catholicism—boredom, family tensions or rebellion, divorce, a bad experience with a priest or nun, a disagreement on moral teachings. But very few leave over true theological issues with doctrine or Christianity, and contemporary research has not linked the pedophile scandals or "rejection by the Church" to a significant movement away from Catholicism.

Research on "Catholic dropouts" showed that most inactives leave during their teens and early twenties, the "find yourself" years. When they left the confines of their parents' home, many rejected their inherited Catholicism as boring and irrelevant. When asked, they may say they have disagreements with the Church on issues such as sexual morality or the ordination of women. But most don't leave angry with the Church; they're just ambivalent. Many say they still pray and believe in God, but a majority (sixty-eight percent of all Catholics) don't think they need to attend Mass to be a "good Catholic."

Who Are They?

Beyond the numbers, here are snapshots of people you're likely to attract to a program that explores the possibility of returning to the Church. The names and details have been changed, but the stories are real and are used with the individuals' permission. The first two stories, however, belong to us, the authors of this book.

> ANNA was raised in a Catholic home where Sunday Mass attendance was never optional. The Catholic faith was an obligation to be met religiously every Sunday and holy day. (Of course, the main attraction for her was the juice and doughnuts served in the parish hall after Mass.)

When she went to college, she met friends who were evangelical Christians, who seemed very serious about Jesus. They committed their lives to serving him and said they had a "personal relationship with him." They studied the Bible and knew a lot about Christianity. Anna had never met Catholics who lived their faith in such a holistic way. It made a deep impression on her. She became "born again" and started attending the local Presbyterian church and a Bible study.

Faced with graduation and not knowing what she wanted to do, Anna became clinically depressed. She found comfort in her new Christian community, but also started wandering back to the Catholic Mass. She began reading about Catholicism, and found that Catholics believe in most of what the other church was teaching about Jesus Christ, but also believed that Christ was really present in the Eucharist. She started listening carefully to the liturgical prayers, and the Mass began to come alive to her in a new way. Most of all, she felt like she was home.

MELANIE was pretty sure she wanted to be Catholic again. She just didn't know how. She was forty-nine years old, and hadn't belonged to a parish for thirty-four years, having left almost as soon as she'd been confirmed. In the past year, Melanie had left her husband and moved five hundred miles away to take a new job. She had filed for bankruptcy to deal with nearly $200,000 in marital debt.

A disagreement with the man she was dating sent Melanie to a therapist. When Melanie told the therapist she'd been raised Catholic and was looking for a spiritual home, the therapist suggested her parish just seven blocks from Melanie's apartment. The parish's bulletin advertised a returning Catholics program, a "place to update your faith as an adult," facilitated by a woman named Anna. It seemed like the best way to explore her concerns and situation.

PAULINE, in her mid-twenties, had been baptized and confirmed. During her high school years, her family moved several hundred miles away from her home-town, and she had drifted away from attending Mass. Now, armed with an advanced degree and on the fast track to her dream job with the federal government, everything should have been perfect. Except it wasn't.

"Something was missing, but I didn't know what," Pauline said. "I had been toying with the idea of going back to church but did not quite know how. I searched for a Catholic church in my neighborhood and found a Landings program. It sounded like exactly what I needed, so I made the call."

JULIA, a Latina in her early thirties, had earned a law degree in her homeland. An attractive opportunity arose for a position with an international aid associa-tion thousands of miles away in the United States. It was perfect for her background, and no one was surprised when she was hired. But then her contract ended.

"I was feeling lonelier than ever without my family, in a foreign country, and without a job for the first time in my life," Julia said. "I was dating a divorced man and that made me doubt whether I was still a good person and a good Catholic. Also, I had always had that thirst for something more, and going to church on Sundays wasn't doing the trick. It just wasn't enough for me to get it, to really believe, to understand, and to have a relationship with God." That was when she saw the notice about the parish's program for inactive Catholics.

What They Need

Dean Hoge, sociologist at Catholic University of America, was among the authors of *American Catholics Today: New Realties of Their Faith and Their Church*. Twenty-five years ago, he conducted research that found demographic and motivational commonalities between returnees and converts.

"We have noted that, sociologically, returnees are a lot like converts," Hoge wrote. "This is especially true of those in their twenties and thirties who are concerned about their marriages or their children....We should not be surprised if the two groups are similar, and evangelistic efforts directed at them would be similar."

In a broader context, many of your parish's inactive Catholics received a typical Catholic education, then stopped coming to Mass in their teens and twenties. Many are children of parents who did not model an active Catholic life. They have little knowledge of their faith and need to re-examine what they know. The Barna Group, a Protestant research group, labels these inactive Catholics as "unchurched" and ripe for evangelization.

The new generation of potential returnees may identify themselves as Catholic, but they have a weak sense of how being Catholic impacts their life. Their sense of Catholicism does not come from their participation in the community or the sacraments, though they know those elements are important. Still, they believe they are still "Catholic," and they can't imagine being anything else, especially when it comes to marriage or baptizing their children.

These adults will be among the first to acknowledge that they need to re-examine their faith. Their eighth-grade confirmation class, long forgotten, didn't give them the resources to know how to live out the challenges of their adult life as active Catholics. As they seek to fill that spiritual void, your parish's outreach to them will help determine if they remain Catholic in name only, or if they renew their relationship with God in a vibrant way and become an active part of your community.

"Feed my lambs...tend my sheep...feed my sheep," Jesus told Peter. "Amen, amen, I say to you, when you were younger, you used to dress yourself and go where you wanted; but when you grow old, you will stretch out your hands, and someone else will dress you and lead you where you do not want to go." ❧ JOHN 21:15–18

Those exploring a return to the Church are stretching out their hands to you, even if that gesture seems ever so slight. When they timidly come to the office to register or inquire about a sacramental occasion, this could begin a process of conversion for them. They have taken the first step. It's not so much that those who have been away don't want to be active again as it is that there's an unspoken fear that they don't know enough, that they're not good enough to be accepted. The smallest effort—a smile or handshake or welcoming word—can make all the difference to these inactive Catholics. Can your parish then offer them a simple way to update their faith as adults and invite them to a more vibrant understanding of what it means to be Catholic? Be a shepherd. Gather up and feed his sheep. They'll be richer for rekindling a relationship with Christ—and you'll be richer for sharing their journey. Let's get started!

CHAPTER 2

Preparing the Pasture

Inactives may feel a lot of fear about coming back to the Catholic Church after years away. Built into that fear is the feeling that the Church may not really want them back. Many returnees have labeled themselves "bad Catholics"; some are divorced, some disagree with Church teachings, some have complicated questions, others just don't know how to "come back."

GETTING UP THE NERVE

One returnee carried the notice for our parish's returning Catholics program in her purse for months until she got up the nerve to contact Anna.

Many potential returnees see the Catholic Church first and foremost as an institution with all sorts of rules, very black-and-white. Their lives aren't that neat, they tell themselves, so why even try to return? Is there a place for them?

Christ issued a clear invitation to all: "Come unto me, all you who are labored, and I will give you rest." What a peaceful and welcoming statement. He didn't say, "Get your act together and then come see me." What the returnee needs to hear is that nobody really is that "perfect" Catholic. Each of us is on a spiritual journey to God. We all have questions. We all struggle.

The Holy Spirit has led these inactives to your door. Can you hear that knock? What a sacramental moment, a sign of God's grace, to bring them together with people, many who are returnees themselves, who know their faith and are willing to take the time to "sit by the well" and listen as Jesus did with the Samaritan woman. What a gift, that your parish can provide a pasture where these adults can find an authentic spiritual community to help them "be Catholic" again.

We talk about "coming back" to the Church, but many returning young adults stopped practicing before their teen years and don't really have a Catholic identity to recover. Their ties and loyalty to our faith are thin, and there are many spiritual options out there for them. These adults aren't passive learners. They have to own their faith by asking questions and engaging in good, honest conversation. You have the opportunity to introduce them not just to the Catholic faith but also to Christ. In the encyclical *Deus Caritas Est*, Pope Benedict XVI reminds us that "being Christian is not the result of an ethical choice or a lofty idea, but the encounter with an event, a person, which gives life a new horizon and a decisive direction."

This generation of inactives will not be attracted by apologetics and argued back into the Church through a presentation of dogma. For these inactives, the teachings are lifeless unless they are communicated by people who are struggling to live them. Sincere Catholics who really love Christ and their faith, and can share that relationship in an authentic way will attract this generation.

Many Catholics today seem to agree that our faith can be practiced without being an active part of a parish community. Sixty-eight percent recently said you don't have to attend Mass every Sunday to be a good Catholic, according to CARA. Many inactive Catholics regard themselves as very spiritual but not religious, because to them "religious" means rules and obligations.

We need to give inactives a reason to become part of us again, to commit to their faith. What an amazing opportunity! Participating in the sacramental life of the Church is essential for a real Catholic identity. We all have our gifts and are called to use them to build up the kingdom of God. The potential returnees who approach your parish are hearing the Holy Spirit call them to go deeper. Resolve that your parish culture will gently beckon them back with programs to meet their needs and provide a spiritual home for them.

A HOLY SPIRIT MOMENT

One returnee drove to Mass twice but just couldn't get out of the car. The third time, her raised Jewish/now Hindu husband agreed to go along.

They sat in the back of the church, trying to be inconspicuous. Of course, the Holy Spirit had other ideas. An usher tapped her on the shoulder and asked her if she and her husband would like to "bring up the gifts." She quickly said "Yes," at which point her husband whispered to her that he wasn't sure what that was.

She said he got quite a kick out of this later, thinking about those Catholics who received their Jesus courtesy of a Hindu.

The First Encounter:
Welcoming or Off-putting?

There is quite a difference between grabbing a meal at the fast-food drive-through window and experiencing a wonderful Sunday Easter brunch with friends and family. Which example most clearly resembles your parish?

In *Excellent Catholic Parishes: The Guide to Best Places and Practices,* author Paul Wilkes comments:

> Excellent parishes have, using Flannery O'Connor's phrase about the considered life, " a habit of being." This ranges from the warm welcome of the parish secretary on an initial phone call to making sure that a first-time visitor at a liturgy isn't a stranger for long....Newcomers are swept into the arms of these parishes, their needs addressed, and they are invited into meaningful parish programs and activities.

This welcoming "habit of being" is essential to the success of any outreach to inactive and returning Catholics, and it may start at your office door. An unfamiliar man or woman is interested in registering for the parish. When asked, most will say they just moved into the neighborhood, but perhaps that moving van actually arrived several years ago. Those in their twenties or thirties probably are there because they are getting married and want a "church wedding" or because they have children who need baptism or religious education. Over half your returnees will be in these two categories. This will be a natural point to invite them back.

This is also a natural point to revisit in a gentle way the attitudes of your staff. For a parish to be truly welcoming to returning Catholics, everyone must embrace their roles as ministers. Establishing your program can help further the formation of even your most loyal volunteers and workers. It's an opportunity to bless and educate each other as well as the potential returnees.

Called to Have a Shepherd's Heart

With priests overburdened and catechists focused on the needs of converts and children, there isn't much time, talent, or treasure to reach out to those who have chosen to remain outside the sacramental life of the Church.

Nonetheless, whether you begin a formal program for returnees or will reach out only to those who come for marriage preparation or the baptism of their children, we urge you to help those in your community examine their feelings about inactive Catholics. What are the attitudes toward people who are "cultural" or CAPE—Christmas, Ashes, Palm and Easter—Catholics? What about people who are considered "Cafeteria Catholics," who disagree with some of the Church's teachings? Does the Church really want such people back?

PREFERRED PARKING?

Even "faithful," "welcoming" parishioners can show their resentment at the influx of Ash Wednesday and Christmas Catholics sitting in their pews and parking in their spaces.

One of us was left momentarily speechless at a parish council meeting the week after one Ash Wednesday. "I don't know why they all have to come on Ash Wednesday," an otherwise pleasant woman in her forties fussed. "I got here fifteen minutes before Mass, and couldn't find a parking place anywhere. I ended up parking in a neighborhood residents-only spot, and got towed. It really made me mad. "

Some believe that people leave the Church primarily because of their own moral failings, and that they walk away from the sacraments and the teachings of the Church willingly. A priest expressed this view in the October 1998 issue of *Envoy* magazine:

> Let us be unflinchingly clear about this while retaining all understanding, mercy, and forgiveness. The great majority of people who leave the Church do so because of moral faults. They are not ready to submit their sins to God and to the Church's judgment and mercy through the sacrament of penance. This unwillingness to ask for God's forgiveness for having offended him leads to rationalization and self-justification. Over time, this will lead to a loss of the virtues of faith, hope, and charity necessary for eternal life. The culpability of these moral faults may be mitigated by religious ignorance, the result of a decades-long failure of the faithful to properly catechize.

This is not the attitude to have when preparing your heart for a ministry for returning Catholics. Sometimes the alienation of these inactives lies firmly at the Church's door. Many returnees come back with complex life stories; they may require annulments or pastoral counseling to help reconcile them fully with the Church. As you do with those already a part of your community who seek such assistance, listen with an open and loving heart and leave the judgment to God. There is little grace—or likelihood of success—in approaching returning Catholics with the attitude that you personally will "save" them.

NO WELCOME MAT HERE

Anna visited a different parish one Easter, when she was still in the process of returning to the Catholic Church. She sat in the back of the packed church and looked forward to hearing the priest preach about the joy and hope of the resurrection. But what she heard brought her to tears.

The priest commented on how full the church was and spent his homily lecturing the parents of those who rarely come to Mass, saying they were endangering their children's salvation. Nothing he said would have made her want to come back to this parish or the Church in general.

"I looked out on those hundreds of blank faces, some of whom may have been as hungry for the Gospel as I was at college, and I silently wept," she recalls. "I wept for those around me who needed Jesus, and I wept for my Church."

Before you proceed with a program, schedule a candid discussion with your parish council and staff about their attitudes toward inactive Catholics. Start by inviting them to share why people they know—family, friends, neighbors—have stopped coming to Mass. (They need not share names or other identifying characteristics.) Ask them what one thing your parish could do to help break down the barriers that stand between the Church and those people.

Next, ask everyone to complete the worksheet that follows, and then move on to an evaluation of your current welcoming procedures.

MY ATTITUDES TOWARD INACTIVE CATHOLICS

Please mark these statements true or false.

1. *People who don't go to Mass are jeopardizing their salvation.*
2. *Most inactive Catholics are angry with the Church.*
3. *If you disagree with the Church, you shouldn't call yourself a Catholic.*
4. *You can be a good Catholic and not go to Mass.*
5. *If you are divorced, you shouldn't go to communion.*
6. *We should invite all Catholics to come back to Mass, but only if they go to confession first.*
7. *There are liberal Catholics and conservative Catholics. All should be welcome.*
8. *If a Catholic feels more comfortable in a Protestant church, he or she should go there.*
9. *We should not baptize a child of parents who don't intend to practice the faith.*
10. *Once a Catholic, always a Catholic.*

After a discussion of the worksheet statements, ask a parishioner who returned to the Church to tell his or her story and initial impressions of the parish. This will give lifelong Catholics greater insight into how the parish is perceived by those outside.

Are You New Here?

Next, it's time to evaluate your welcoming process. Start at the beginning, with the way phone calls to the parish office and the registration process are handled.

Ask yourself these questions:

- Are your front office staff members, usually the first people inactives meet at the parish, trained to be helpful and welcoming? Do you have a real person answering the phone, or do you rely on voicemail? Many returning or inactive Catholics are hesitant to leave messages.

- Does your parish have a procedure for following up with new families? Is there a way you can minimize paperwork and simplify the connection between ministry leaders and newcomers interested in getting involved? It is a big turnoff to express interest in volunteering and never be called to help.

- Is there any followup with the newcomers, a letter or a phone call to invite them to attend Mass again or attend a special event at the rectory? Consider using your seniors, Knights of Columbus, or Legion of Mary in this capacity.

- Is there a welcoming event where new members can meet each other and other parishioners and learn about the parish offerings?

- When newcomers walk into the church for the first time, do the ushers greet them? Are the ushers or a welcoming committee available after Mass to answer questions about the parish and offer a newcomer information packet?

Do you offer coffee and doughnuts on an occasional or ongoing basis after Mass? Encouraging on-site fellowship can be complicated if parking lots need to be cleared for the next Mass. But providing a treat and tables for visiting facilitates a welcoming atmosphere that benefits the entire parish.

Consider putting together a short action plan—no more than five items—that can be accomplished with minimal effort or money. Examples might include placing a welcome sign on the front door or offering cookies at the reception desk. Gather the participants again in two or three months, and celebrate the progress made, no matter how small.

BEING NEIGHBORLY

One parish has different ministries host the popular coffee/doughnut hour between Masses. Each ministry makes a short presentation to the captive audience, active and inactive, to share what it does.

At these events, encourage parishioners to talk with people they don't know. It is lovely for newcomers to walk out feeling somewhat connected. Once, Anna sat next to a young mother and her child at a hospitality hour. The woman was newly arrived from Iowa; her husband was in the military and worked on Sundays. Anna told her about the mother's playgroup on Tuesdays, and she came the next week. Two years later, she was running the playgroup.

The Invitation

Chapter 3 details ways in which you and your staff can reach out to inactives to share information about a formal program.

But a first step, even before you commit to a course or discussion series, may be a simple bulletin announcement of support:

Welcome Inactive/Returning Catholics

If you are a Catholic who has been away from the Church, know we are thinking about you. We are glad you are here and invite you to be an active part of us again. If you would like more information on our parish programs and ways you can get involved, please contact (name) at the parish office.

Even without a specific program, this is a way to both sensitize your community to the fact that there may be strangers in the assembly and to give inactives a specific person in the parish to call to chat about their situation.

One of the most popular days for inactive Catholics to attend Mass is Ash Wednesday. These "Ash and Dash" Catholics tend to get their ashes and sneak out before communion. A celebrant announcement (sample below) before the liturgy may encourage some return visits.

We know that many of you may be visiting our parish for the first time. We are glad that you are here and welcome you. If you have been away from the Church, we invite you to be an active part of us again. Please see the bulletin for more information or call the church office and ask for (name).

These small gestures of recognition may encourage someone to pick up a bulletin and come back again. The Holy Spirit works in mysterious ways.

Adult Faith Formation: Feeding the Soul

Many inactives say they stay away because they don't know enough to be Catholic. New parents are especially interested when they think about passing their faith to their children. All many remember from their religious education days is singing "Day by Day" and sneaking out to the convenience store for candy. The idea of returning to that form of study is unappealing to these thirsty returning Catholics.

What is called for is a shift away from adult education that mirrors the school model where students passively receive information from a teacher to adult faith *formation*, a real engagement through the learning experience. Consider emulating the RCIA model: let adults share their stories with other adults. What young adults in particular need is mentoring by older adults with credibility and sharing with others who have had similar life experience. Catechesis and adult conversation happen best in a setting where our hearts can engage one another.

Help your baptismal and marriage preparation ministers in particular to understand the needs of returning Catholics, since these sacramental preparations will be the first adult experience many of them have with the Church. The formation programs should allow for dialogue, not just about the sacrament but also about the demands of living a faithful Catholic life. Keep the groups small, no more than six couples per session. Resist the temptation to consider it "good enough" if the couples or parents just show up for each discussion. Warmly engage them and draw them into the conversations.

Try to get the participants to talk about themselves and their relationship to the Church. Ask about the parish where they grew up and why it is important to them to be married in the Church or have their child baptized.

Can a challenge be incorporated into the training with an invitation to become more involved in the parish life beyond just the baptism day? Then, if you have a special program for returning Catholics, can the formation ministers be sensitized to offer a discreet invitation to those they meet that might benefit from it?

All elements of adult formation can have an eye toward the evangelization of returning Catholics if your parish ministers know their audience and see themselves as shepherds.

The Warm Embrace

Many people expect the worst when they decide to come back after a long time away from the Church. Remember when the prodigal son approached his father after spending all his inheritance? He had already rehearsed a speech acknowledging he was unworthy of his father's love and shouldn't be called his son. But the father ran to meet him and embraced him. There was no talk of the past sins, only a warm welcome back to the family.

If your parish can be a welcoming pastoral setting, then once the inactive finds you, the Holy Spirit will do the rest.

WELCOMING THEM HOME

One returning Catholic finally got up the courage to go to confession after thirty years away. She girded herself for the lecture that she expected from the priest.

When she said, "It has been thirty years since my last confession," the priest said kindly, "Welcome back. The angels in heaven are celebrating today." She has been an active Catholic ever since.

How to Help Them Find You

Once upon a time, parishes that wanted to bring inactives back to the fold would slip a note in the bulletin at Christmas and Easter, buy a small ad in the local newspaper, and count on the Holy Spirit to do the rest.

Then the Internet came along, and everything changed.

Now, your parish may not need to buy print ads. But it does need to know about things like search engine optimization. The majority of inactives living within your boundaries most likely are Web-savvy adults. Nearly ninety percent of inquiries for the suburban Washington, D.C., parish we serve come via e-mail, generated from the Internet.

While the Internet may seem impersonal, it has obvious advantages for returnees and for your parish. E-mail is quick, easy, anonymous, and available 24/7. Little risk is involved; the inactive Catholic doesn't have to call the parish office and talk to a real human being, and you know that the caring, compassionate facilitator of your choice is going to respond to every e-mail received. As ministers, we need to go where the inactives are because, like it or not, it has to be all about the inactives before they can be all about Christ.

OVERCOMING THE INTIMIDATION FACTOR

Inactives who visit CatholicsComeHome.org can get answers to their questions about the Church before they are directed to the site's parish finder. "Being able to explore questions and concerns of the faith in the comfort of one's own home is much less intimidating than having to get these initial questions addressed face-to-face at a parish-based inquiry program," said Susan Gerdvil, director of communication for Catholics Come Home, which works with dioceses to re-engage inactives. People who explore the site "are much more comfortable seeking out their local parish (or) entering a parish inquiry or RCIA program," she said.

We asked a few twenty- and thirty-something returnees about this approach. Some liked the idea of being able to dig around a Web site before having personal contact; others wanted their own questions answered and said they didn't think they would have gone on to rekindle their faith if they'd come across this site while looking for information about being Catholic again.

Your Parish and the Internet

Having an effective Internet presence isn't an option for today's parishes. It's estimated that by June 30, 2008, nearly seventy-five percent of North Americans had been online.

Entire books and Web sites are devoted to the essentials of effective site design and on how to optimize your site so that its pages show up near the top of specific search engines. We won't try to replicate their efforts in a single chapter. But it is important that you discuss with your Webmaster the words those mulling a return would use to find your program specifically. It isn't expensive or complicated. It is important that you take advantage of this opportunity.

Here are the results of some recent searches using Google, the most popular Internet search engine:

"return to the Catholic Church": 6.6 million

"returning Catholic": 5.5 million

"ex-Catholic": 43,500

"recovering Catholic": 32,100

What does this mean? It means that long-running returnee programs such as Coming Home and Landings and other entities have determined that inactives are more likely to search for assistance with the words "return to the Catholic Church" or "returning Catholic" than with words such as "ex-Catholic" or "recovering Catholic." And, through the use of content analysis, meta-tags, links, site maps, and other techniques, Google has learned searchers are most likely to find useful content on pages with such words. (For help with improving your site's visibility in Google Search, have your Webmaster check out https://www.google.com/webmasters/tools/docs/en/about.html.)

There's no sin in taking advantage of what the big guys have already learned when it comes to keyword searches. But just adding "return to the Catholic Church" or "returning Catholic" to your site's content won't get your parish ranked very high in those millions of matches. That's why it's important that your content, especially for your returning Catholics program, also includes location-specific information that the searcher might use, such as your city, area code, or ZIP code.

Remember those millions of results for "return to the Catholic Church" and "returning Catholic"? We ran those same searches with the names of key cities in states that the Pew Forum on Religion and Public Life says have a disproportionate Catholic population.

PHRASE	MATCHES	NOTES
"return to the Catholic Church"	6.6MM	
"return to the Catholic Church" CityA	178	no local Catholic church programs on the first page
"return to the Catholic Church" CityB	21	first match is a parish ministry contact list that hasn't been updated since 2005
"return to the Catholic church" CityC	3,240	no local Catholic church programs on the first page
"returning Catholics"	5.5MM	
"returning Catholics" CityA	564	several links to a national program; no local programs on the first page
"returning Catholics" CityB	269	first match is a local parish; others on the first page are national programs or local programs more than a thousand miles away
"returning Catholics" CityC	380	first match is the diocesan Web site; no links there or elsewhere on the first page to local programs

Surely, more than two of the more than five hundred parishes in those dioceses have courses or discussion groups to help light the way back for inactive Catholics. Simply adding keywords to attract inactives plus a city name could do so much to make the parishes' sites and programs more visible.

THINK LOCAL

Imagine what the prodigal son would have done if his father had sent servants to direct the son to read a book or consult other media of the day rather than running out himself in a welcoming spirit. Imagine how many sheep would have been saved if the shepherd had painted a directional arrow toward shelter rather than going after the sheep personally.

We respect and admire greatly the national programs that have been so successful in ministering to returning Catholics. You'll find information about each of them at the end of the book, and adopting one of their programs may work best for you and your parish.

But whether you use a tried-and-true approach, develop your own ministry, or decide to simply include a "welcome inactives" item in the bulletin occasionally, we urge you to designate a priest or lay minister as the parish contact point for inactives. A special e-mail address for this contact should be listed on your Web site and ministry directory. This person should be a good listener and have the pastoral skills and knowledge of parish resources to answer inquiries promptly and help assist the returnee in plugging into parish life.

The Invitation

Start where the inactive is likely to start: your home page. Consider a hotlink on your home page that reads "Interested in returning to the Church" or even "Become Catholic again" (even though we all know that anyone who is baptized is Catholic, regardless of the vigor of that belief).

The parish we serve is an example of a simple but effective Web outreach to inactives. Type "returning Catholics" and "Arlington, Virginia" in a search engine, and the St. Charles Borromeo "Contact Us" page, including an e-mail address for the parish Landings program, is the first match. If returning Catholics decide to click to the home page (www.stcharles-church.org) first to find out more about the parish, they are met on the left bar by a permanent "Return to the Church again" hotlink to a brief description of Landings, two testimonials, when the next session begins, and Anna's phone number and e-mail address.

Whether or not you plan a formal program, language such as this would be appropriate:

We welcome you to our parish Web site. If you have been away from regular Mass attendance and would like to learn more about our faith community and the Catholic Church today, please contact (name, phone number, and e-mail address).

If you plan to offer a course, don't overload the page with a week-by-week discussion list. The goal is to be inviting. Consider adding something like this to the above:

At a (number)-week course that begins (date), you can discuss your questions and concerns with other returning Catholics. Pre-registration is required.

If at all possible, include brief testimonials from two or three people who rekindled their faith as a result of your course.

Don't put information on the Web site about where and what time you meet. The goal is to get those contemplating a return to reach out to the facilitator via a "safe" communication vehicle such as the phone or e-mail. Specifics can be shared when you meet with interested inactives one on one before the sessions begin so that you can determine whether this is a good fit for both them and your program. The personal connection at that point is key. By the time returnees have looked at your site and e-mailed or called you, they are mentally ready and eager to take the next step. Rejoice in that step, and set the banquet table for them.

Bulletin and Newspaper Announcements

The great thing about announcements in your bulletin and at Masses is that they cost your parish nothing. The bad thing is that unless they're well timed and well constructed, you won't reach potential returnees.

We all know that inactive Catholics are most likely to feel the tug back at Ash Wednesday, Christmas, and Easter. You might consider starting your program two to three weeks after one of these key dates so that announcements can appear in the bulletin during the high-traffic time and perhaps the week before and the week after. Remember, if the people you're trying to reach aren't in the pews that day, even Pulitzer Prize-winning text won't help.

An effective announcement might look like this:

We welcome you to our parish today. If you have been away from regular Mass attendance and would like to learn more about our faith community and today's Catholic Church, please contact (name, phone number, and e-mail address) and check out the bulletin and our Web site. At a (number)-week course that begins (date), you can discuss your questions and concerns with other returning Catholics.

One of the best celebrant announcements we ever heard went something like this:

It's great to see so many of you today. Thank you for coming. We hope to see you again soon. For those of you who wish to explore your faith after being away from regular Mass attendance, a (number)-week course begins (date). In those sessions, you can discuss your questions and concerns with other returning Catholics. See the bulletin and our Web site for more details.

Please resist the temptation to make comments such as: "God expects you in these pews every Sunday, not just twice a year" or "The parking lot was really jammed today. I can't wait until things are back to normal next week." Even if you think you're making a joke, those who don't come to Mass regularly won't take it that way.

You might also consider having your facilitator, a team member, or a program "graduate" make a brief announcement. Inactives may find it difficult to hear these words coming from a priest or parish staffer whom they may believe has never been alienated from God. This doesn't need to be a lengthy witness, just the announcement above along with a statement that the person went through the program a year ago and found it helpful on his or her personal faith journey.

This will be a real encouragement for inactive Catholics, to learn that there are people just like them who left the Church and who are now active, valued members of the parish.

UNDERSTANDING THE INACTIVE MIND-SET

One of us saw this poster on public transit during Advent: "Invest in someone who guarantees a good return."

Then, after a Renaissance-era painting of Mary, Joseph, Jesus, the Magi, and the shepherds came a list of ten churches with their Metro stops and street addresses—and the dates and times people could go to confession.

It broke our hearts because:

- *Confession/reconciliation is the sacrament inactives fear most. A better tactic would have been to include Christmas Day Mass times.*

- *The listings included no Web sites or phone numbers for the churches or for the diocese.*

- *The "guarantees a good return" language, rather than being clever, reinforces the erroneous baggage that non-practicing Catholics (and non-Catholics in general) may have about a requirement that we do service to "earn" our way into heaven.*

A better strategy might have been a headline along the lines of "Come Home for Christmas" or "Share the Real Meaning of Christmas," along with contact information for the parishes—and any programs they have for returnees.

WHAT ABOUT TV?

Television time can be expensive, and production costs can be even higher. But this medium may be the right approach for some parishes.

Catholics Come Home works with dioceses on advertising to drive inactives to CatholicsComeHome. org where they can access resources.

"We have had tremendous success reaching inactive Catholics by airing CatholicsComeHome.org commercials repeatedly during popular secular TV programming," said Susan Gerdvil, director of communication for the entity. "When they return to the Church for an inquiry program, [inactives feel] comfortable using the commercial as a starting point of discussion as to why they are returning: 'I saw a CatholicsComeHome.org ad on TV and that's why I'm here. Can you help me with the steps I need to take to re-enter the Church?'" Gerdvil said as many as 6,000 inactives returned to parishes during a three-week TV campaign in a test diocese.

Other Tactics

Free newspaper ads. Public service announcements on the radio. Bulletin board announcements at coffee shops and bookstores. Online blogs and videos and podcasts. Signage in front of your parish. The possibilities are limitless. But it's likely the amount of time, talent, and treasure you can spend on this ministry is extremely limited.

One or all of these strategies may work to attract inactives to your parish—or they may not attract a single person. Before embarking on any of them, we suggest you ask yourself and your staff:

- What do we know about the demographics of inactive Catholics within our parish boundaries?
- What are the key information sources for people in those demographics?
- What key messages would help them overcome inertia or fear and rekindle their faith life ("Plan Your Catholic Wedding Right," for example, or "Come Home for Christmas")?
- What action can we encourage them to take (provide phone numbers, Web sites, e-mail addresses)?

EVANGELIZATION CARDS

CatholicsComeHome.org, an online entity that works with dioceses to answer inactive Catholics' questions and then directs them to their local parish, offered this example:

"One parish in Burbank, California, ordered over 1,100 CatholicsComeHome.org Evangelization cards, similar in size to business cards, and challenged their parishioners to share the cards with family and friends that they know who are away from practicing their Catholic faith."

Word of Mouth

What's the cheapest, most effective way to bring inactive Catholics home? Through the invitation of family, friends, or neighbors. Encourage your parishioners to give out flyers advertising your returning Catholics program to inactive Catholics they know. Personal invitations do work. To share one example, one older returnee hadn't been to Mass since her grandmother's funeral twenty years before. The only reason she heard about our program was that a kind neighbor gave her the flier. She knew the active Catholic cared for her, and she didn't want to disappoint her, so she came. Not only did she complete the whole series, but at the end of the eight weeks, the returnee had her marriage validated in the Church in front of her returning Catholic friends, with her neighbor as the witness. There wasn't a dry eye in the place, as the healing love of God had worked a miracle for this returnee.

Also key is fostering a parish culture that's so vibrant and inclusive that your members discuss (or forward via e-mail) with friends and neighbors a homily that resonated; speak with joy about their ministry involvement; and bring non-parishioners along to the lectures, panel discussions, dances, dinners, and other events.

Research has shown that most of today's younger inactive Catholics got that way not because they had a serious theological issue or rupture with doctrine, but because they were ambivalent about the culture at their parish and didn't bother to look for another one.

You know the demographics of your parish's geographic boundaries (or, if you're not sure, check out the QuickFacts section at www.census.gov). Do your ministry and education offerings reflect the interests of the overall community? This might be a good time to survey the assembly to determine which activities should be strengthened or added and which should be downgraded or eliminated. For more ideas on fostering a welcoming attitude, please see Chapter 2.

Found!

Congratulations! A number of inactive Catholics have responded to your outreach efforts. However, don't be discouraged if only a few inactives commit to participating in your program. Our large (more than thirty-five hundred families registered), transient parish located less than a mile from two urban college campuses averages about five to seven returnees per session, with two sessions per year. The ideal small group including team members is eight to ten.

If, however, you have only one or two returnees for more than a session or two, consider re-evaluating your communications strategy and whether a full program is appropriate for your parish demographics. Or, you may prayerfully decide to focus your outreach on godparents and brides and grooms. In any event, do know that even if the program serves only one or two returnees, you are providing a real blessing for those individuals, a place for them to rediscover their faith and move forward on their journey.

WHAT IS SUCCESS?

Catholics Coming Home Founder Carrie Kemp says: "We do not measure success/failure in terms of how many return (many attend the series more than once, sometimes years apart!), but rather in terms of whether the seekers leave with a feeling that they will always have a church home with us, regardless of where they are on their journeys."

Be sure to ask each person who contacts you how he or she heard about your program, and track that information. If, for example, fifty percent found you via an Internet search, forty percent read about you in the Christmas bulletin, and ten percent heard about the program from a parishioner friend, you know you probably don't need to spend much effort going forward on transit ads or radio spots, even if actual space and time didn't cost the parish anything.

Next, we'll look at the crucial one-on-one pre-session meeting between the potential returnee and your facilitator.

CHAPTER 4

The Meeting

Minister's Reflection (Anna)

As I approach the coffee shop, I am always a little nervous. The person I'm meeting is thinking about a return to the Catholic Church. Some have been away only a few years; for some, it's been half a lifetime. Some come after much thought and with trepidation; others decide to contact me on a whim. Either way, I may be the first "Church" folk the person has spoken to in years.

In concept, this meeting is supposed to provide more information on our eight-week discussion program to see if it's a good fit. But the most important purpose is for the person to see that I am not a grumpy Church Lady, ready to drag him or her off to the confession box. My job is to warmly welcome these folks back and listen to their stories of how God has brought them to this point.

This is an important moment for this Catholic, a sacred moment, and I listen reverently. Catholics don't easily talk about their personal faith; we are private people and don't have the language that evangelicals do. Nevertheless, it is surprising to me how we are ready to open up when invited to do so. Most returnees, once they realize that I am not there to condemn them, are very ready to talk about their lives and answer spiritual questions. The Lord has knocked on their hearts, and their contact with me is their initial "Yes."

As I approach the door, I say a quick prayer to the Holy Spirit, that he will be glorified in our conversation and that I, as a minister, will learn to get out of the way of what he wants to do in this person's life. I enter the coffee shop and begin to look for a short lady with brown hair and a black blouse.

Returnee's Reflection (Melanie)

It was a God thing that I ended up in a Catholic Church in August 2005, and it was even more of a God thing that the bulletin had a little item about a program for returning Catholics. I had to see the item two or three times before I mustered up the courage to send an e-mail to Anna LaNave. She called me within a couple of hours, and we agreed to meet at a coffeehouse a few nights later.

I knew who she was the minute she walked in, and not because she was the one wearing a green-striped shirt, as she said she would. No, as she chatted briefly with a friend before she headed over to my table, I could feel her warmth, her peace, her serenity. I wanted that. And I knew she could help me get it.

Anna didn't bat an eye when I told her it had been nearly thirty-five years since I had received the Eucharist and that, really, I wasn't sure I'd ever felt a part of the Church growing up, even though something was surely tugging me back now.

"Well, let me tell you a little about our program," she said. "It's a safe place to ask questions about the Church today to figure out if you fit in. There's no pressure. We hope the answers help you find a place in the community, but that's your decision. It runs for eight weeks for two hours on Wednesday evenings."

Why a Pre-Session Meeting Is Essential

When someone considering a return to the Church has taken the time to contact you and seems interested in committing to the program, it is important to set up a face-to-face meeting before the session starts. This pre-session meeting with the lay leader is critical because:

- It will give you an opportunity to provide a warm welcome back. Catholics who have been away frequently view the Church as a cold institution, and your smiling face counters that image.

- It shows that your parish is serious enough about the program to set aside a special time to meet with the potential returnee.

- It gives you an indication of where returnees are on their journeys and whether they are truly ready to explore a return to the Church. If someone can't make a coffee meeting, it doesn't bode well for his or her commitment to the program.

- It eases the returnees' nervousness and will increase your program's attendance rate. People will know at least one face—yours—when they walk into the first meeting, which will help relax them.

- It lets them open up to someone about where they are in their faith journey and see that they will not be judged for their questions or doubts.

❧ It provides an opportunity to determine whether the returnee will be a good addition to the group. Some people are in the midst of a divorce or are suffering from depression. Your program will not be able to provide professional help, such as counseling, but you may be able to provide direction to the right resource. Gently suggest that the person may not be ready for the program at this time, but that you will contact him or her in the future.

At minimum, have a phone conversation with each inactive and get as much background as you can before the first session. If you decide that the person might be a good fit, invite him or her to attend the first meeting and agree to meet immediately afterward to discuss whether the person should continue.

Hold a separate meeting with each person, with the possible exception of engaged or married couples who are considering coming to the program together. Returnees often will share very personal information, such as past marriages or parental abuse, at this initial meeting. They have taken a huge step in their spiritual journey by contacting you, a step they may not have discussed with anyone else. Honor their privacy.

Don't be surprised if most of your list of potential participants is female. It's been our experience that women are more proactive about pursuing a faith journey that involves sharing stories. We've also found that professionals of all ethnicities tend to come to our program. We don't get many young parents or stay-at-home moms, probably due to babysitting concerns. And we've noticed no difference in the type of ministry desired by returning Catholics whether they are Caucasian, African-American, Asian, or Latino.

WHAT CAN HAPPEN

If you don't meet with an inactive in advance, you may regret it later. Anna was unable to meet with one young woman in advance, but encouraged her attendance anyway. The woman's anger about the unfaithfulness of her devout Catholic mother, who had just divorced her father, monopolized the group discussion during successive meetings. Other returnees were caught up in her crisis as a result. If Anna had met with this woman ahead of time, she would have pointed her toward pastoral counseling rather than the returning Catholics program.

Where and When to Meet

It's tempting to meet at your church office, but that is not a good idea. Meeting at church is much too formal and intimidating. It says, "I am the church minister here to help you."

Meeting at a coffee shop close to your church can put people at ease. Returnees don't have to be worried that someone they know will see them going into a church; they could be meeting an old friend at a public place.

Let the returnee's schedule dictate the time/day as much as possible, and give yourself about forty-five minutes or so for the meeting. Respect the person's time, and do not cancel if humanly possible.

Make sure you tell the returnee what you will be wearing so he or she can identify you. Consider always wearing the same shirt or jacket so it's easy for you to remember what to tell the returnee. Get there a few minutes early if you can and take a quiet table in the corner.

Pre-Session Meeting: What Happens

The meeting's stated "purpose" is to share information with returnees about your program and see if the program is a good fit for them. From the minister's point of view, the main reason is to let returnees tell you about their lives and why they are being called back to the Church at this time. You want them to know that the Church is concerned about them. Your main job is to listen and be interested, which isn't hard to do.

This is a sacred time. Another human being is letting you have a little glimpse into his or her unique soul. As you listen, try to find commonalities between your faith story and theirs to share. They are not alone in their stories. As you let them talk, you will see their shoulders relax. They are being heard by the Church, and the Church seems interested in them. As they tell their story, you will hear in their words how God has been active in circumstances and people to bring them to this moment of a possible return to the faith.

Your program has a sacred responsibility to help those considering a return to connect their life story to Christ, who is actively seeking them out and loving them back to himself. The pre-session meeting is not the time for you to make these connections. The process will do that. Just know that God is at work and let the Holy Spirit do its thing.

After a returnee finishes his or her story, transition into discussing the program. Ask if the person has any barriers to his or her return to the Church, or any specific topics he or she would like discussed during the program. Explain that the meetings will include time to ask questions about the Church, and that all views will be respected. Many people will appreciate an adult approach to faith formation, where discussion is encouraged and not discouraged. This will allow the group members to freely wrestle with their doubts together.

Ask the person to complete a sheet with contact information. Then provide a list of the topics to be covered during the sessions, and some reflection questions for the first week.

Explain to the potential returnee that continuity and mutual respect is important, so everyone is asked to attend the majority of the sessions (ideally, all of them). Share that the members will be creating a small group community, and that includes sharing faith journeys. Let the person know that all members will be invited to share their stories, and familiar faces are helpful in doing so. Compliment the person about the way his or her story was just shared with you, and provide assurance that details that would make him or her uncomfortable to disclose may be kept private.

If people say work and family obligations will keep them away for several sessions, gently suggest that this may not be the right time for them to join the program. Some lives are at a very busy place; to those folks, a returning Catholics program may seem like just another obligation that would be difficult to manage. Offer to contact them before the beginning of next session.

If it doesn't come up in the returnees' stories, ask in a nonjudgmental way whether they are currently attending Mass. Some may not have set foot in a Catholic church for many, many years. Encourage everyone to attend a Mass before your program starts. This is a first step in reconnecting with faith and with seeing the Church in action today. Suggest that they sit in the back if they are concerned about going. They may not be ready to go to the Eucharist, but they do need to reacquaint themselves to being part of the parish community. If they have been to Mass recently, ask them about the experience.

At this point, consider giving the inactive a resource book as a gift. A list of recommended titles appears in the Appendix. You'll want to provide something that is light on theological terms and realistic on issues inactive Catholics face.

Pre-Session Meeting Wrap-up

As you come to the end of your meeting, ask the returnee if the program seems like a good fit. Most will say this is exactly what they need at this point.

Let the person know precisely where in the church the meetings will be held and provide details about parking or public transportation. Advise him or her that the meetings will start promptly and end promptly, to respect everyone's time.

As you say good-bye, the returnees usually will say they are looking forward to the meetings. Let them know that you are too. You, as a minister, know that God can do a mighty work with a heart that is open to him, and you are excited to see what the Holy Spirit has in mind.

CHAPTER 5

Building Your Program and Team

W hether you've cast the net for inactives or they've arrived on your doorstep for sacramental or other reasons, you now have an interested group. Now, what do you do for them?

With resources scarce, it is tempting to try to plug them into existing parish programs. Many inactive Catholics who return with "faith questions" are directed to the Rite of Christian Initiation for Adults (RCIA). But we don't believe this is the appropriate place for them. Though their needs may be similar, they are already Catholic by virtue of baptism and need a place for discernment, not straight catechesis or sacramental preparation. In addition, some returnees may have personal issues with the Church to work through. Their presence in the RCIA may not help them—and it might confuse others.

A specific program for returning Catholics shows that your parish acknowledges their existence and wants to help with their unique spiritual needs. What should it look like?

Formal programs tend to fall into one of two categories:

ꙮ informational sessions with no requirement for registration and no vetting of attendees in advance. These sessions are very informal, once or as a series, and last a couple of hours. Typically, key "hot button" issues raised by the attendees or by the moderator, usually a priest or lay minister, are discussed, such as "Reconciliation" or "Marriage and Annulments." There is no commitment to participate beyond that gathering, though attendees are invited to schedule an appointment with the priest or minister to help their re-entry if their issues are complicated.

ꙮ six- to ten-week faith formation classes that are topic-specific (sometimes sacramentally based) and similar to a small-faith sharing group. The facilitator prescreens participants and keeps attendance to no more than eight to ten. The weekly meeting includes story sharing and prayer; the topic discussion includes an element of basic catechesis. In many cases, the groups involve both returnees and a team of active (welcoming) Catholics, many who may be reverts themselves.

Brief descriptions and contact information for a number of these programs appear in the Appendix.

Picking a Style

Which is right for your parish? If you are unsure how many returnees are in your area, the informal approach may work. Our parish used this strategy one Christmas with meetings titled "The Church Is Listening" and "The Church Has Changed." The sessions were modeled after the Catholics Coming Home program. Many of the attendees had received fliers from friends and neighbors. Our pastor was present at both sessions and was available for questions and answers. For those who needed a quick answer to a question, such as a couple who wanted to ask about starting the annulment process, it was ideal.

The downside to this approach is that anyone can show up, including those who come to make trouble or who are especially angry and would be better served by one-on-one pastoral counseling. At one of our sessions, a practicing Catholic pro-life activist challenged an inactive woman who expressed concerns about her pro-choice stance and her Catholic identity. They got into a verbal conflict that set all the participants on edge. The active Catholic was asked not to come to the next session, but it was too late. The inactive Catholic did not return.

If you go this route, we suggest you also consider sponsoring a more formal formation program. You can invite anyone who attends the general session to join you, explaining that discussions will be geared to the questions and needs of returnees. It's been our experience that younger adults in particular are looking for this type of solid spiritual food.

The downside to this approach is that some people may be reluctant to commit to an evening every week for several weeks to discuss faith issues with people they don't know. This is why the pre-session meeting is so critical. It allows the facilitator to determine the interest level of each possible participant and emphasize that while the inactive may try things out at the first meeting, after that, attendance is extremely important as the participants will be building a community. It is important to see the same faces each week as inactive Catholics will then feel more comfortable speaking honestly about his or her faith. Once returnees attend the first session, they are usually hooked.

ABOUT LANDINGS

Our parish's sessions are based on the Paulists'
Landings *programs, established in 1986 in response
to Pope John Paul II's emphasis on evangelization
for the coming millennium.* Landings, *which has
served more than 70,000 people in thirty-five U.S.
dioceses, derives its name from the notion of providing
returning Catholics with a landing place, a safe spot
to touch down. Its goal is to facilitate inactive Catholic
discernment of their place in the Church and to help
them return to the sacraments. See the Appendix for
contact information for* Landings *and other formal
programs.*

*At our parish, with our large young adult
population, the* Landings *program has been enhanced
over time to include a stronger catechetical element
during the topic discussions and greater interaction
with the parish itself through a presentation by the
director of adult faith formation, one by our pastor,
and a home Mass at the conclusion.*

Whether you choose to develop your own program with
the tips we've shared or decide to work with an existing program, understand that helping returnees talk about their lives
and the role of the Catholic faith in their past and assisting
them in identifying any barriers to full reconciliation if they
desire it are key.

A program like this is not showy or complicated. It says,
"We want to get to know you and walk with you during this
period as we talk about the faith together." While you will encourage folks to attend Mass regularly, many will not be ready

for that when the session begins. That's all right. Let them meet active Catholics who can be their spiritual friends. In this age where religious talk is avoided as taboo, your program should be a safe place where it is encouraged. Your meetings become a sacred haven for all involved.

Who's There?

If you select the formal program approach, the small group dynamic is critical. Try to keep the size to no more than six returnees and no more than four team members (all active Catholics) to welcome them back.

You've already pre-registered the returnees and met individually with them to be sure they are committed to the program. But how do you select your shepherds?

Here are some traits team members should share:

- ACTIVE IN THEIR FAITH. Team members should be nice to be around, not angry or harboring any unresolved issues concerning their own relationship with the Church. If they are in the midst of their own personal crisis, this is not the time to ask them to focus on ministering to others. It's also important that the members understand that while your parish is sponsoring the program, it is Christ they serve. The goal is to help the returnees rekindle their spiritual lives and encourage their re-entry into the Catholic faith, not to convince them that your parish is the best one in the diocese.

- ACTIVE IN THEIR LISTENING. Many returnees have been hurt by representatives of the Church and need to have that hurt acknowledged. Listening, rather than being a Church apologist, is key. This isn't about convincing them to returning to the Church; it is about being Christ to them, loving them back to communion with the body of Christ.

- ❧ **ACTIVE IN THEIR SHARING.** Catholics who have been through a program such as this will be aware that you will be asking them to share their spiritual story—within reason because, after all, they are there to minister to the attendees. The sessions are not for them, but for the returnees. If you have facilitators who have not been through such an experience, they may need some time to prepare to share appropriately about their journey.

- ❧ **ACTIVE IN THE SPIRIT OF MINISTRY.** Successful ministers will recognize that the Holy Spirit, not they, is at work here. Even if no one returns to active status after the program, your job is to be faithful to the process. The team members' ministry is to plant the seed; they may never see it blossom and should be comfortable with that.

While it's important that team members share those traits, we encourage you to embrace as much diversity as possible in age, ethnicity, sex, marital status, economic status, and so on. In this way, returnees may find it easier to believe there is diversity within our Church. You also may have different devotional personalities in the group. Great! Returnees may enjoy hearing about a variety of Catholic customs, since they may never have grown up with them.

The best team members are usually those who have had returning experiences themselves and are prepared to talk candidly about their spiritual journeys. This example also provides those who finish the program with an example of service as team members if they so desire.

If you can find about three to five faithful folks to help run your program, you are in good shape. This is a quiet ministry and doesn't need a lot of fanfare once it begins. This number also will not overwhelm the returning Catholics. You will also be able to rotate your team members among sessions, and so avoid burnout.

Before the session begins, gather the team to discuss how the format will work and who will do what at the first meeting and throughout the session. If the members do not know each other, do some formation of your own through faith sharing and other fellowship activities. Have each of them share the story of his or her spiritual journey. Pray together for the Holy Spirit to assist you in this sacred ministry. You and they will be blessed to have a front-row seat as your small group, a group of strangers, begins to bond and relax with each other.

What Does It Look Like?

Consider running your session for two hours for eight or so consecutive weeks. For our parish, Wednesday evening works well. For others, Saturday morning or Sunday afternoon may be optimal. It will all depend on the lifestyle of your parish and of the returnees within your boundaries. For us, fall and spring sessions work; again, depending on your parish, more or less frequent sessions or keying the timing more closely with the post-Advent or post-Easter period, may work. Don't be afraid to experiment until you have the right fit.

Look for a warm place on church property where you can set up a circle of chairs and a table to the side for refreshments. If possible, steer clear of a classroom; people seated around a table tend to remain formal and reserved longer than a situation where nothing but perhaps a bench with a lighted candle separates them. Nametags are helpful for the first few weeks. Have the team members arrive early so they can greet the returnees individually and spend a few minutes chatting casually with them.

A PASSIONATE LAY LEADER

If you are going to start this ministry, it is imperative to find the right person to lead it. Though it is important to have a strong team, it is critical to have one person be the public face for the ministry. This person needs to be passionate and committed to this sensitive ministry. He or she should be a good listener, someone who lets others lead the conversation and is genuinely interested in getting to know the returnee.

This person is not a fixer, but a minister, committed to prayer. He or she should be able to return phone calls and e-mails on time, and know when to pursue a returnee and when to back off. It's helpful but not critical for this person to have a theological/pastoral background, but he or she should at least be able to direct the returnee to the right resource. The person must be aware of the diversity of returnees' backgrounds and be committed to keeping the program focused on the authentic teachings of the Catholic faith, and not his or her ideological perspective on the teachings. Without someone passionate about leading this ministry, it will become something else on the director of religious education's plate and it will not survive. You need someone who believes in the process and is willing to provide the time and energy needed.

We strongly recommend limiting the presence of a priest. There may be a few returnees who are angry with the Church because of the negative experience with a priest or a nun. It may be very intimidating to them to have a priest in the room. At our parish, the pastor presents on sin and reconciliation midway through the session after the group has had an opportunity to gel. By this time, some returnees are ready to set up private meetings with him. Encourage the priest to leave time for questions at the end. In a small group setting, in the company of people who are now their friends, returnees frequently are ready to accept that priests can be human and approachable.

SUGGESTED SCHEDULE

Welcome/Icebreaker

Opening Prayer

Storytelling

Hospitality Break

Discussion Topic

Brief Topic Presentation by Facilitator/Team Member

Intercessory Prayer/Closing Prayer

Storytelling

A key element for such a program is the returnees' sharing of their spiritual journeys. Many have never shared so personally at this level about their Catholic faith.

Questions you might ask the returnees to consider in developing their stories include:

- ❧ What are your earliest memories of Catholicism?
- ❧ What and/or who were your early spiritual influences?
- ❧ Why did you stop practicing?
- ❧ Why are you thinking of coming back, and what if any barriers do you face?

This is one benefit of having met one on one with participants before the session starts (see Chapter 4): each returnee has already told his or her story once, and thus may be more comfortable sharing it in the small group.

At the first meeting, invite each returnee to sign up to share his or her story at a future session. You or a team member should talk about a personal journey the first week so that the returnees have a model to follow. If team members were once inactive themselves, it provides real encouragement for the returnees. Suddenly, they are no longer alone with their concerns.

Explain that the group's role is to listen silently, then to reflect on how the returnee's story touched them. Many will have had the same experiences and some of the same questions as the storyteller, which is very affirming for the group. It builds a sacred space for everyone, with confidentiality and a nonjudgmental attitude emphasized.

This is a very powerful part of the session and a key starting point for processing conversion. For many, this is the first time they have placed their life story in a spiritual context:

Where was God in that or this? How is he leading me now? Ideally, the returnees will come to see that they may have been in a relationship with God without acknowledging it. God has been a part of their life journey from the very beginning, and now, by intentionally thinking about their Catholic faith, the returnees are taking a positive step back into deeper communion with God. Like all of the Church, returnees are all on a journey to him, and the events of each life have significance. Faith is not just about Church but about a relationship with God; salvation is not something to be obtained but something to be experienced as we grow closer to God. Life is a process of two steps forward, one step back, but always on a path guided by God's grace.

TEARING DOWN WALLS

The most powerful moments we have had during our meetings have come when a person takes a risk and is very vulnerable in his or her story. One woman in her late twenties, whom we will call Lynn, read from her journal about her "fears" as part of her story. She had written about fears for her future, about whether she would ever marry, and about doubts she had about her abilities. Lynn wrote that she knew the doubts were from the devil; fear is not from God, she said. Suddenly, many around the circle spoke up and agreed with her, saying that they too were very fearful, especially about trusting God. It was quite amazing and the group really bonded after that moment. True fellowship had been achieved because a person had been willing to take a risk. This was all the work of the Holy Spirit.

Praying Together

We strongly urge you to open and close each session with a prayer. We ask for volunteers to lead the opening prayer, and people can pray in any way they feel led (music, prayers off the Internet, devotionals). *Landings* calls for a reciting of the Newman prayer or another formal prayer at the session's end.

Consider adding time of intercessory prayer to help the returnees become comfortable with the practice. Following the model of the prayers of the faithful, we offer a time when people can ask for prayer for a concern, and then the group responds, "Lord, hear our prayer." While team members may be the only ones who voice prayers in the beginning, by the end, most returnees also are willing to offer up their requests.

During one session, a returnee received a cell phone call. Her boyfriend's mother had been diagnosed with cancer. She was very shaken, and we encouraged her to go home if she needed. We told her we would pray for her, and after she left, we all took some time to ask for comfort for her and for the woman. Here was a demonstration for the returnees of the power of the body of Christ, interceding for a hurting member. It was a very special, authentic moment for all of us.

Discussion Time

While storytelling is the most powerful tool for conversion in your program, the discussion topics and presentations by your team will help the participants understand what being Catholic means. In the next chapter, we'll share a sample line-up—and questions to expect from the returnees.

CHAPTER 6

Feeding the Flock

Many of the excellent returning Catholic programs developed in the 1980s had the same image of inactives: wounded and angry, hurt by the Church in some way. The thought was that all the Church needed to do was apologize to these inactives and gently lead them back to the sacraments.

It is true that many people, especially the veterans of Catholic schools in the 1950s and '60s, may have some horrible tales to tell. Other inactives were hurt by priests who refused to baptize children or by Catholic parents who disappointed them. If your parish's boundaries include a large number of older Baby Boomers, those who were confirmed pre-Vatican II or in its immediate aftermath, this ministerial approach may still resonate. These returnees remember what it was to be Catholic, and you just need to invite them back and help them update their faith.

However, the majority of returnees in many parishes will be adults in their twenties and thirties. They are not angry with the Church, just ambivalent. The children of Baby Boomers, these young inactives participated in religious education, received at least some of the sacraments, and then stopped going to Mass. Why? Because they were ambivalent. Religion, God, and the Church didn't seem relevant to their lives. When they think about re-engaging with the Church as adults, they want to reconnect with our teachings, this time with the freedom to question and discuss them. They want to know what the Church believes so that their Catholic identity will be lived authentically. They are not resistant to good catechetical information, they are hungry for it—and your program needs to feed them.

Your Program: A Roadmap

In Chapter 5, we discussed the storytelling dimension of weekly small group meetings. After a hospitality break, we recommend discussion of faith topics. This segment starts with the facilitating team member asking a question about the topic. Then each person is allowed a few minutes to comment on the question. Then, the team member will present a brief presentation on the Church's teaching on the topic. After the presentation, the returnees are invited to ask their own questions.

It is important that the team members provide knowledgeable, reasoned thoughts about Church teachings, not simply their opinion or experience. They need to provide insight into why we as Catholics believe what we believe, and be prepared to answer questions about those beliefs. Available resources for solid information include the *Catechism of the Catholic Church*, Scripture, books, and many Web sites (including those listed in the Appendix). We encourage team members to prepare handouts to go with the discussion. You might think that lay Catholics, noncatechists, may be intimidated by the task of teaching the faith. But all Catholics are called to be able to articulate the faith, and our team members have embraced the challenge.

The national returning Catholics programs provide prescribed topics for each week's discussion. While our parish's program is based on the *Landings* meeting schedule, we have adapted the topics significantly to reflect the needs of the returnees to whom we have ministered. We have included a suggested reflection question to begin the session, and finish with some possible returnee questions that we have heard, which your team facilitator should be prepared to answer.

Remember, your program's goal is a real engagement, first with Christianity and then with the way in which the Church nourishes that faith. The order of topics is crucial to the reflection process.

WEEK ONE   WHO IS JESUS?

WARM-UP: *If all religions are possible, why are you a follower of Jesus?*

It may seem remedial to start with Jesus, but returnees may not even be sure he was a real person. This can be a challenging discussion. Many inactives do not identify being Catholic with being Christian (a follower of Jesus). Use this opportunity to talk about who Jesus Christ is and what it means to follow him. Talk about our faith not only as a list of things to believe, but also as a relationship with Jesus to be lived. We challenge the returnees to read through one of the Gospels on their own, to meet this Jesus anew.

It's helpful if the presentation discusses the creed and the Church's faith in Jesus as fully divine and fully human. Also, explain about Jesus' uniqueness in human history and his role in salvation. This discussion sets up the framework for the rest of the program.

QUESTIONS YOU'RE LIKELY TO HEAR

? *Is the evidence about Jesus Christ reliable?*

? *Isn't being Catholic different from being Christian?*

? *I never thought about Jesus much, I pray to God. Is that okay?*

WEEK TWO   ARE YOU SAVED?

WARM-UPS: *Tell me about your last experience at a baptism. What do you say if an evangelical Christian walks up and asks you "Are you saved?"*

Since some returnees have been exposed to an evangelical understanding of salvation, it is important to talk about what Catholics believe. We recommend sharing the Church's teaching that salvation is not gained in a moment of commitment, but begins with baptism, is affirmed through confirmation, and is a lifelong process of living in a graced relationship with God. Share that Catholics believe it is not by faith alone that we are saved; that by cooperating with God's grace, we actually become more like Christ as we reflect his love to others. We were created to live with God forever, and we are in the midst of a personal transformation to prepare us to meet him face to face.

Be aware that some participants may be considering a return precisely because our Church provides a clarity of teaching on religious and moral issues, something that is not always present in nondenominational Christian churches. They may be hungry to better understand the Church's teaching and doctrine. It is important that it be presented clearly and from primary sources as much as possible.

Share a basic definition of why we have sacraments—that they are physical and spiritual gifts of God to us to help us grow closer to God—and that the Church is the vehicle to help us live out our faith as Christ's adopted sons and daughters. Explain that at baptism we are welcomed into the family of God and become a member of the body of Christ (the universal Church) and at confirmation we receive a special anointing of the Holy Spirit, to be witnesses of Christ to the world.

QUESTIONS YOU'RE LIKELY TO HEAR

? *Why do Catholics have to do good works while Protestants seem to know they are going to heaven?*

? *What about those good people who are not Christian? Does the Church say they are going to hell?*

? *Does the Church accept the baptism of another Christian Church as valid?*

WEEK THREE WHAT IS CHURCH?

WARMUP: *When you think of "Church," what first comes to mind?*

Say the word "Church" and returnees think of a cold institution, the priests, the pope, and so on. In this discussion, explain that we are the people of God, the Church, and we are here, as the Church, to serve God and neighbor. Consider having the parish's director of religious education lead this discussion about the body of Christ.

It's key to share that the Church needs the gifts and talents of each of us to help bring the kingdom of God to this world. The Church is not just about servicing its own members but is also about mission, reaching out to the world and bringing Christ into our homes and workplaces. We are called by our baptism to live the faith authentically every day, not just on Sunday.

If there's time, this is a good week to discuss how Catholics use the Bible, that we have specified Old and New Testament readings for every day of the year. Share that while we do not read the Bible literally, as some fundamentalists do, the Church teaches us that "it contains the authoritative truth that God wishes to teach us." Explain that we believe the Holy Spirit teaches us through Scripture and Tradition (the teaching office of the Church/Magisterium). Encourage the returnees to pick up a copy of the *Catechism of the Catholic Church*.

QUESTIONS YOU'RE LIKELY TO HEAR

? *How can the Catholic Church say it is the "true" Church? Isn't that a little arrogant?*

? *What about those books like the Gospel of Thomas that didn't make it into the Bible? Didn't the Church manipulate the canon to get the books it wanted?*

? *Are Church teachings ever wrong?*

WARMUP: *What are your experiences of the Mass and the reception of the Eucharist?*

Other than the Week One dialogue on Jesus, this discussion will be perhaps the most challenging you will encounter. Many inactives are very surprised that Catholics view the Eucharist as the real presence of Jesus Christ, not something symbolic. Encourage them to listen to the words of the Eucharistic Prayer with this in mind, that Jesus is giving us himself and that we are called to respond to that gift by saying "Amen" to our Christian faith and what we believe.

For others, the Eucharist is at the center of why they are seeking a return. One of us has two cradle Catholic-turned-evangelical-Christian friends. Even though they are respectively ten and thirty years removed from Mass attendance, both speak longingly of the Eucharist as the thing they miss most. For some returnees, the concept of again sharing in the body and blood of Christ may be overwhelming. Be prepared for questions—and perhaps some tears. Many may be in situations, such as nonsacramental marriages, where full communion is not possible at this time. The facilitator should be sensitive to these issues.

We explain that at the Last Supper, Jesus gave us himself in the form of bread and wine to nourish us and to be present to us in an intimate way. Jesus lives in us, by the presence of the Holy Spirit. In this way, the Eucharist is not something we "get," but something we experience in community.

Many parishes schedule a tour of the church as part of this discussion to share the symbolism of the Mass and to help inactives better understand our worship life and why we do the things we do at Mass.

QUESTIONS YOU'RE LIKELY TO HEAR

? *Why doesn't the Catholic Church allow non-Catholic Christians to accept communion? It seems a little rude.*

? *If I am divorced, but not remarried, can I go to Communion?*

? *When should I refrain from going to Holy Communion?*

? *Is it still a mortal sin if I miss Mass on Sunday?*

WEEK FIVE   SIN, CONSCIENCE, AND FORGIVENESS

WARMUP: *What is sin and why do we have the Sacrament of Reconciliation?*

This is an ideal topic for the pastor or other ordained religious to present. In our parish, the pastor explains the Church's understanding of reconciliation and how one goes to confession or reconciliation. If the returnees have been away for a while, the face-to-face option may be totally new to them.

Ask the presenter to first talk about sin as a barrier to love and our relationship with God and others. It's helpful to explain that while God forgives all our sins, we frequently have trouble forgiving ourselves and that the sacrament of reconciliation helps us to remember God's grace.

At this, the halfway point of the program, returnees may feel ready to reconcile themselves with participating fully in the Church. Encourage them to make a private appointment with the pastor if they wish for private reconciliation. If your parish offers a communal reconciliation service (during

Advent or Lent, for example), this may be an attractive option. One group of returnees at our parish made plans to go together to such a service as a support for one another.

If your priest is the presenter, please allow time at the end of the presentation for an "Ask the Priest" no-holds-barred question and answer time. This informal atmosphere offers returnees an excellent opportunity to ask any difficult questions that may not have been fully addressed during previous sessions.

QUESTIONS YOU'RE LIKELY TO HEAR

? *How often should I go to confession?*

? *What is the difference between a mortal and venial sin?*

? *What if I don't remember my act of contrition?*

? *Why do I have to talk to a priest, if God has already forgiven me?*

WEEK SIX   THE LAST THINGS

WARMUP: *What have you learned through the sickness or death of someone you love?*

At our parish, this is the week we talk about the problem of suffering and the importance of the Paschal Mystery in understanding our destiny to be with God. In Christ, we have a God who has suffered in solidarity with us, and we have the hope of the resurrection. We also talk about the Sacrament of the Anointing of the Sick and healing.

The issue of nonbelievers and hell always comes up, as does the question of why bad things happen to good people, and vice versa. Emphasize that God wants all to be saved and that the Church makes no pronouncements on the ultimate destiny of anyone. We have the assurance of God's love for us and can rely on that love to be perfectly just and merciful. Emphasize that if we desire a relationship with him in this life, we will find complete fulfillment of that desire in the next.

This is another week where you may hear questions about what Catholics believe vs. what fundamentalist or evangelical churchgoers believe. Listen carefully to the emotion behind the questions rather than the language used, which may sound confrontational. For these returnees in particular, understanding the promise of salvation may be a key issue.

QUESTIONS YOU'RE LIKELY TO HEAR

? *Why do we pray to the saints and Mary? Why not go directly to Jesus?*

? *Is there still a purgatory and what exactly is it?*

? *Why does God choose to listen to some prayers for healing and not others?*

? *What about my wife/husband who died and wasn't Catholic? Will I see her/him in heaven?*

WEEK SEVEN   VOCATION

WARMUPS: *What calling (vocation) has God given you? How are you living it out?*

Returnees should see their lives as an adventure in faith, with God giving each of them special gifts to serve the body of Christ. They may be surprised to hear that service to God goes beyond the religious life to being a faithful spouse, excellent parent or child, friend, singer, writer, teacher...the list goes on and on. Challenge the returnees to think about their own gifts and talents, and how they can become active in the Church's mission of building the kingdom. Ask them to examine how God is calling them to serve their parish, their families, and the larger world.

QUESTIONS YOU'RE LIKELY TO HEAR

? *Why is marriage a sacrament in the Catholic Church?*

? *What is an annulment, just divorce Catholic-style?*

? *Is there a vocation to the single life?*

? *Why aren't there married priests and female priests?*

WEEK EIGHT   HOT BUTTON ISSUES/WHAT'S NEXT?

WARMUP: *What teaching of the Church do you struggle with and why?*

You may wonder why we recommend waiting until the end to discuss issues such as birth control, abortion, and the Church's position on homosexuality. Fear? Not at all.

We have saved these moral hot buttons as well as the culture of life and social justice concern to present them holistically. Emphasize that a faithful Catholic has an informed conscience with which to think about these topics. Share that the teachings of the Church are Holy Spirit-inspired and thus need to be seriously considered. You may find that many of the inactives have accepted secular views of these topics without having explored the reasons behind Church teachings.

Don't be surprised if the groundwork you've laid in the previous seven weeks means there are few questions at this point. That's a sign that the inactives are truly becoming engaged, adult, thinking Catholics who have spent some time on their own and with recommended resources pondering these issues.

Close this final session with the participants reflecting on their time in the program and, if they wish, sharing where they are in the returning process. Many will be very honest. Also, ask for written evaluations of the program so that it can be continually improved.

QUESTIONS YOU'RE LIKELY TO HEAR

? *Can I still be a practicing Catholic if I disagree on Church teachings such as abortion and birth control?*

? *Can someone be a homosexual and be Catholic?*

? *Are female Catholics who had abortions excommunicated?*

Closing Mass and Potluck

Some programs suggest ending with a rite or a retreat for the participants. We'd advise against a public ceremony; after all, their return is private and sacred. They are not new

Catholics, but returning Catholics. But a celebration is in order!

If your diocese permits, consider inviting your pastor to celebrate Mass in the home of one of the team members. This can be a lovely intimate time that further demonstrates Christ's presence everywhere, not just within the parish church. In this safe setting among friends, people will feel comfortable receiving the Eucharist or simply asking for a blessing. After the Mass, it is nice to end with small gifts for all the returnees, such as rosaries or spiritual books. This is also an opportunity to introduce them to that Catholic standard, the potluck meal.

This is an ideal time to ask the participants to consider being on the team for the next session, to help those who are seeking to be welcomed back just as they were. Typically, one or two will eagerly step forward.

Others will ask about parish ministries and ways to continue learning more about the faith. Chapter 7 and the Appendix suggest ways to reach out to the returnees post-session and provide resources.

The Soul at Rest

What do the returnees find in a program like this? Our prayer is that we provide a safe haven for them to hear the voice of the Good Shepherd and to experience his love again through a ministry of the Catholic Church. By focusing on storytelling and adult discussion with an intentional catechetical component, you encourage an adult engagement with the faith and begin to form an adult Catholic who knows what it is to be committed to Christ and an active part of his body, the Church.

Will everyone who attends your program return fully to the Catholic Church? No. Conversion is the work of the Holy

Spirit and is very mysterious. It is ultimately a conversation of the heart between God and his child, and the Church, through you and your team, who have added a loving component to the discussion. All you can do is be faithful to God's call to Peter: feed his sheep. We pray that through your efforts, inactives will find in the Catholic Church a place where that nourishment can continue and where their soul can find rest.

In the final chapter, we will share ways in which you can feed the flames of those whose souls caught fire as a result of your program.

RETURNEE CHECK-IN

Melanie, Pauline, and Julia share their mid-course thoughts:

MELANIE: *My single strongest memory is of the facilitator talking about God putting an imprint on us all at baptism. Overall, the theme of Christ's love each session gave me the courage to try to be Catholic again.*

PAULINE: *I think the thing that stands out most with me was the sense of community. I definitely felt the presence of God in each session and through the community, I knew that God had called me back.*

JULIA: *I remember the warmth and openness of the team members, willing to discuss any question or concern humbly and nonjudgmentally. I was amazed and fascinated to hear other people's struggles, so different and yet so similar in essence to mine, everyone looking for something to calm that thirst for God.*

CHAPTER 7

Feeding Their Fire

You know all those jokes and witticisms that begin: "There are two kinds of people in this world..."? Well, it's been our experience that there are three kinds of people who complete courses to reacquaint themselves with their Catholic faith:

- The first kind decides all this Church stuff isn't for them, not right now, anyway. These folks go on to explore other faiths, or decide a deeper relationship with God is not a priority at this point. They may or may not rediscover Catholicism at a later date. You've sown the seed, and the next step is theirs.

- The second kind becomes the type of Catholics who fill your pews. They attend Mass regularly and participate in the weekly offertory collection. They send their kids to your school or catechetical classes, but don't get heavily involved in parish ministries. In a spare moment, you might wonder about their spiritual life, but then you put that thought aside. They've come to the well, and how deeply they are drinking is between them and Christ.

🖐 The third kind catches fire. They volunteer for every committee and come to every parish event. They challenge the ways you and your congregation have always done things and don't speak your liturgical language. They amuse and bedevil you and your staff until they burn out or find a ministry that values and nurtures their flame. As their shepherd, they look to you and to the parish for guidance in finding that special place.

Ultimately, Catholics who return are adults and will make their own decisions about how publicly engaged they wish to be in their faith. Your last "official" duties as the shepherd of such a program will be to check in with the participants a few months later for feedback on how to improve what you do, and to provide information about opportunities for deepening their relationship with Christ. While we are one in the Spirit, no one service opportunity will set all of your participants on fire. Share as much as you can about parish and diocesan ministries and related Catholic movements and organizations so that the returnees can find the community that best fits them.

Now What?

Our parish's sessions are held in the Upper Room. Without fail, at least one person at the final meeting before the home Mass looks around and says something like this: "What am I going to do without you guys? I'm going to miss coming here every Wednesday. I'm not going to know what to do with myself."

Someone usually asks if the attendees can keep meeting as a small faith-sharing group or a book club. Sometimes, there's a suggestion of a reunion in a few months. But as in most places, life happens in our parish. People move in and people move out. They get married and have children, or the children leave the nest. Within a year or so, that little group that was so connected for six to eight weeks and was so committed to staying connected is usually no more.

It may be quite a culture shock as the returnees leave the warmth of your weekly meetings and now must find their niche in the general parish community. At first, it may be quite a disappointment. They will feel lost without their small group. They will meet Catholics with whom they disagree, or they will run into priests or staff members who don't seem to have time for them. But just like any family, we learn to live with one another, forgive one another, and hopefully come to love one another. The parish is our school of love.

That's why your program facilitator's final official gift to the returnees is the gift of the Holy Spirit, a little nudge to get these believers out of the Upper Room and into the larger body of Christ. Whether it's through fellowship at Mass or engagement in a particular ministry, it's important that they understand that they and their rediscovered faith are called to live in community, to share with others the gifts the Lord has bestowed upon them.

Ways to Do It

Your parish may have an annual or twice-yearly fair after Masses at which ministries share information about the services they provide or the help that they need. If the timing works, you may wish to schedule a special coffee session for your returnees that coincides with a ministry Sunday. That way, the members get to see people they know and be exposed to what may be the next step in their faith journey.

Similarly, if your parish has a directory of ministries that includes descriptions and contact information, consider providing a copy to all participants at the end of your last session. Be careful to limit this outreach to sharing a resource document. Don't pass around a sheet on which the returnees must indicate the volunteer activity of their choice; after all, the returnees are in our program to determine whether they wish to rejoin the body of Christ, not to be recruited for service. Your primary role is to provide a warm, nonthreatening place for them to share their concerns and fears about the Church and then, and only if they desire, to gently shepherd them back to a more active Catholic life.

We've talked elsewhere in this book about parishes where ministries take turns hosting the weekly post-Mass coffee and doughnuts fellowship. If your parish does this, make that the group's homework one week, to go to fellowship and share what was learned.

If your course is in session during Advent or Lent, ask if the attendees are interested in a group project—such as wrapping gifts for the Giving Tree or ushering at the Reconciliation service—that will bring them into contact with other members of the parish. This exposure can help broaden their base of parish acquaintances beyond returnees and let them experience how enriching it is to be part of the body of Christ in action.

We've found it effective to have the parish adult faith formation director give a brief talk on church life during one of our sessions. She doesn't do an active solicitation for ministry involvement, but it's helpful for those who wish to be involved later to have a contact point at the parish office.

The facilitator also may wish to reach out individually by phone or e-mail to the attendees two to three months after the course is over. This isn't the Grand Inquisition; don't ask if they've been going to Mass or participating in the sacraments on a regular basis. Just let each person know he or she has been in your thoughts and prayers, and ask if you can be of any further service. This may be the point at which you hear comments such as "I'd like to get more involved in social justice," or "Can you tell me how I'd become an usher?" You then can link the person with the appropriate ministry representative.

FROM CONVERSION TO DISCIPLESHIP

It's natural that some attendees will want to share their newfound fire with others who are walking part of their own road. Some may volunteer to serve on the team for the next session of your returning Catholics program. Others may find their calling as RCIA sponsors.

Catholics Coming Home founder Carrie Kemp said: "It is significant to note that while we began with a focus on assisting inactive Catholics in their relationship with the Church, it has evolved most prophetically into a conversion process leading to discipleship. The returning seekers become committed, involved parishioners who participate in the life of the faith community."

A Step Beyond

It's no surprise that each parish takes on the tone of its assembly and, to a degree, its pastor. No one community can meet the needs of all its parishioners. For example, your parish may be heavily involved in pro-life ministries and Project Rachel; the parish across town may focus on assisting the elderly. A third parish within the diocese may see outreach to the homeless as its main ministry.

We are mindful that marriages must be celebrated in the parish of one of the spouses and that other major sacramental occasions typically are celebrated within the boundaries of the parish in which one lives. We're not encouraging parish shopping, especially by those who have recently returned to Catholicism. God doesn't preside over a popularity contest. However, if a returnee has a strong interest in a ministry that is not a focus of your parish, there are ways to keep this new member engaged and fed.

A good place to start is to refer the returnee to diocesan programs. One of us grew up in a diocese that today has 128,000 baptized members living hundreds of miles apart in communities ranging in population from a few hundred to 100,000. Yet the diocesan Web site provides a robust variety of ministries and ways to participate in them, from active outreach to prayer chains to phone trees. Even in the most rural of areas, a returnee can connect with others interested in the same type of service.

Participation in national Catholic organizations will meet the needs of other returnees. For example, the Knights of Columbus and Catholic Daughters of the Americas provide strong bases of charity, fraternity, and unity for men and women respectively. Cursillo, with its "group reunion" weekly small faith-sharing model, may be appropriate for those who wish to continue their formation in an informal setting. The Legion of Mary, with its weekly work projects, may suit others. A list of the Web sites for these organizations and others follows in an appendix.

We strongly encourage you to provide information about resources that feed not only the returnees' desire for physical service but also help them develop their knowledge of the Bible and the Church's teachings. So often, education for returnees stopped with Confirmation class or even with preparation for First Communion. We've heard more than one person say with some embarrassment, "I've got a second-grade faith." Help them find the discussion groups, classes, and books that will change that.

RETURNEE CHECK-IN

Anna, Melanie, Pauline, and Julia share their current vocations and spiritual thoughts:

> **ANNA** *recently completed her master's degree in pastoral studies at the Washington Theological Union. Her dissertation focused on conversion and the returning Catholic. Since 2003, she has facilitated the Landings program at St. Charles Borromeo Church in Arlington, Virginia, and recently became the regional coordinator for Landings International, where she is heading up a new Washington, DC office for the Paulist ministry.*

> **MELANIE** *is on the* Landings *team at St. Charles and has served on the parish council and Web and development committees. She is divorced and annulled and has completed Chapter 13 bankruptcy debt repayments. Melanie is active in the Arlington Diocese's Cursillo organization. Writing for a Catholic blog and contributing work to devotion collections are among her ministries.*

> **PAULINE** *is involved in Cursillo and led a young adult faith group for more than a year. She currently is an RCIA sponsor and a* Landings *team member. "God has brought me places in my life*

that I would not have imagined and as a result I have learned to trust in God and the greatness he has planned for me," she says.

JULIA *is a Landings team member and RCIA sponsor. "This faith journey never ends," she says. "It gets better with time and effort. I still have a lot of issues that I want to work on in my life, but I'm very happy to say that my relationship with God is not an issue anymore, but a blessing for me."*

On behalf of returnees everywhere, we thank you for your willingness to reach out to those who feel alienated from our Church for whatever reason, yet know in the back of their minds that they remain Catholic in their hearts and souls. May they, you, and your ministry be forever blessed.

APPENDIX

We've provided you with the basics for setting up your own parish program to assist inactive Catholics in returning to the Church. In this appendix, we provide information about some of the better-known formal programs as well as a list of links and books that may be of interest to your team and returnees.

PROGRAMS

ALPHA was launched more than twenty years ago by Holy Trinity Brompton, an Anglican church in London, as an introductory course in the Christian faith. The Lay Catholic ministry *ChristLife*, an apostolate of the Archdiocese of Baltimore, supports the use of Alpha in the United States supplemented by the video series *Catholics Listening to God*.

   WEB SITE: www.christlife.org

   E-MAIL: info@christlife.org

   PHONE: (410) 531-7701

   MAIL: ChristLife, 12280 Folly Quarter Rd., Ellicott City, MD 21042

CATHOLICS COMING HOME began in Minneapolis, Minnesota, in 1984, founded by Carrie Kemp. The six-week series is grounded in sound principles of Catholic evangelization, beginning with a welcoming community and allows seekers to reconsider their faith journeys from new perspectives of God, church, and their own experience.

E-MAIL: cKempKairos@aol.com

PHONE: (651) 457-5427

MAIL: 460 E. Annapolis St., West St. Paul, MN 55118

CATHOLICS RETURNING HOME is a six-week RCIA-like process that encourages inactive Catholics to resume an active practice of their faith. A six-week sequence of topics on the basics of Catholicism is conducted in a non-judgmental support-group format. Sally Mews is the founder.

WEB SITE: www.catholicsreturninghome.org

E-MAIL: ssmews@msn.com

PHONE: (847) 855-0629

MAIL: 15925 W. Anna Dr., Wadsworth, IL 60083

COME HOME was begun in 1986 in New York City by the Franciscan Friars. Other parishes that have used the program include Buffalo, New York; Boston, Massachusetts; Raleigh, North Carolina; Little Falls, New Jersey; and Wilmington, Delaware.

E-MAIL: comehome@stanthonyshrine.org

PHONE: (617) 542-6440

MAIL: Father Flavian Walsh, OFM, or Father Donan McGovern, OFM, St. Anthony Shrine, 100 Arch St., Boston, MA 02110

LANDINGS was designed more than twenty years ago by Paulist Father Jac Campbell to welcome those who wish to investigate returning to the Church. The program is in use in more than eighty-five dioceses in the United States, Canada, England, Scotland, and Singapore. In early 2009, the PNCEA launched a new program called *Awakening Faith, Reconnecting with Your Catholic Faith,* a small-group process for inactives.

> **WEB SITES:** www.landings-international.org; www.paulist.org/namerican/evangelization.htm; www.awakeningfaith.org
>
> **E-MAIL:** pncea@pncea.org; Joan Horn, joanlandings@aol.com (Landings) Anna LaNave, landingsdc@yahoo.com (Washington office)
>
> **PHONE:** (202) 832-5022; Joan Horn, (979) 690-7953 (Landings) Anna LaNave, (202) 269-2550 (DC office)
>
> **MAIL:** North American Paulist Center, 3031 Fourth St. NE, Washington, DC 20017-1192

RELATED SERVICES AND RESOURCES

AMBASSADORS OF CHRIST: BUILDING RECONCILING COMMUNITIES, a formation institute of the North American Forum on the Catechumenate, is directed at parish leaders. It explores the mystery of reconciliation; invites participants to reflect on the vision and process of conversion and reconciliation; explores an understanding of a reconciling community rooted in initiation; and examines present processes and future possibilities for reconciling ministry in the parish.

WEB SITE: www.naforum.org

E-MAIL: info@naforum.org

PHONE: (202) 884-9758

MAIL: North American Forum on the Catechumenate,
125 Michigan Ave. NE, Washington, DC 20017

CATHOLICS COME HOME partners with dioceses to implement advertising campaigns that drive viewers to visit CatholicsComeHome.org. There, returnees can find answers and information related to the reason they may have fallen away from the Church. A parish finder helps people find their local parish. If your parish is interested, ask your diocese director of evangelization or the bishop's office to contact Catholics Come Home.

WEB SITES: www.CatholicsComeHome.org
www.CatolicosRegresen.org (Spanish language)

E-MAIL: info@catholicscomehome.org

PHONE: (678) 585-7886

MAIL: 560 W. Crossville Rd, Suite 101, Roswell, GA 30075

ONCE CATHOLIC, a Franciscan Friars program, seeks to help people reconnect with a local Catholic faith community via the Internet. Their Web site, www.OnceCatholic.org, offers eight chat rooms, information, and referrals to programs within the Church in the United States.

WEB SITE: www.OnceCatholic.org

PHONE: (513) 241-5615, ext. 116

MAIL: St. Anthony Messenger Press, 1615 Republic St.,
Cincinnati, OH 45210

Catechism of the Catholic Church, 2nd Edition. New York: Doubleday, 2003.

United States Catholic Catechism for Adults. Washington, DC: United States Conference of Catholic Bishops, 2006.

LINKS OF INTEREST FOR FACILITATORS AND RETURNEES

American Catholic • WWW.AMERICANCATHOLIC.ORG

Catholic Digest • WWW.CATHOLICDIGEST.COM

Catholic Education Resource Center • WWW.CATHOLICEDUCATION.ORG

Catholic Online • WWW.CATHOLICONLINE.ORG

Center for Applied Research in the Apostolate • HTTP://CARA.GEORGETOWN.EDU/

EWTN, the Global Catholic Network • EWTN.COM/INDEX.ASP

Living Faith Daily Catholic Devotions • HTTP://WWW.LIVINGFAITH.COM/INDEX.PHP

Mass Times around the World • WWW.MASSTIMES.ORG/DOTNET/CAMPAIGN.ASPX

New Advent • WWW.NEWADVENT.ORG/INDEX.HTML

Pew Forum on Religion & Public Life • WWW.PEWFORUM.ORG

Pew Research Center • WWW.PEWRESEARCH.ORG

U.S. Conference of Catholic Bishops • WWW.NCCBUSCC.ORG

The Vatican • WWW.VATICAN.VA

CATHOLIC CUSTOMS & TRADITIONS
A Popular Guide
GREG DUES

For 20 years now Catholic Customs & Traditions *has been a bestseller—and it is still going strong. Our **NEW 20th Anniversary edition** celebrates and affirms this classic resource in this very special hardcover edition.*

From Candlemas to the Easter candle, through relics, Mary, the saints, indulgences, the rosary, mystagogia, feast days, laying on of hands, and much more Greg Dues presents the richness of Roman Catholic heritage. Presented in a clear and engaging manner with well-researched historical and theological grounding, this is a timely and useful resource for anyone with interest in the history and traditions of the Church.

224 pages | $19.95, hardcover | 978-1-58595-771-2

***ALSO AVAILABLE IN PAPERBACK* | 224 pages | $14.95 | 978-0-89622-515-2**

OUR CATHOLIC SYMBOLS
A Rich Spiritual Heritage
MICHAEL J. DALEY

Here Michael Daley offers a fascinating and informative overview of our symbolic language. He breaks these down into core symbols of Catholicism, symbolic persons from Scripture, saints as symbolic persons, virtues, Christians symbols, and symbols of the Mass. This is a must-have resource for anyone who teaches about the faith—or just wants to know more about it.

120 pages | $12.95 | 978-1-58595-753-8

BASICS OF THE CATHOLIC FAITH
BILL, PATTY, AND LISA COLEMAN

Readers can refer to this handy resource for a wealth of information about Jesus and his teachings, the customs and traditions of the Church, Catholic prayers, saints, and devotions, and much more.

144 pages | $12.95 | 978-1-58595-109-3